DONNA KARAN

Designing

an

American Dream

DONNA KARAN

Designing

an

American Dream

Sherill Tippins

 GARRETT EDUCATIONAL CORPORATION

Cover: *Donna Karan.* (Peter L. Gould/Images, Inc.)

Manufactured in the United States of America

Edited and produced by Synthegraphics Corporation

Library of Congress Cataloging in Publication Data

Tippins, Sherill.
  Donna Karan / Sherill Tippins.
    p. cm. — (Wizards of business)
  Includes index.
  Summary: A biography of Donna Karan, whom Women's Wear Daily has
called the hottest designer on Seventh Avenue.
  ISBN 1-56074-019-1
  1. Karan, Donna, 1948- —Juvenile literature.   2. Women fashion
designers—United States—Biography—Juvenile literature.
3. Fashion designers—United States—Biography—Juvenile literature.
[1. Karan, Donna, 1948- .   2. Fashion designers.]   I. Title.
II. Series.
TT505.K37T56   1991
746.9′2′092—dc20   91-32784
[B]   CIP
                                                            AC

Contents

Chronology for **Donna Karan**

1948	Born on October 2 in Long Island, New York
1966– 1968	Attended Parson's School of Design
1968	Began working as a summer intern at Anne Klein and Company
1969	Married Mark Karan on March 17
1971	Named associate designer at Anne Klein
1974	Gave birth to daughter Gabrielle on March 17; became chief designer at Anne Klein
1983	Successfully launched Anne Klein II; divorced from Mark Karan and married sculptor Stephan Weiss
1984	Started her own company, Donna Karan New York
1985	Called "the hottest designer on Seventh Avenue" by *Women's Wear Daily*; launched a line of accessories and a licensing division
1988	Introduced DKNY, a less expensive line of women's clothes
1990	Company revenues reached $130 million; named Women's Designer of the Year by the Council of Fashion Designers of America

Chapter 1

"I Always Knew I'd Be Something!"

One day in 1969, a young woman named Donna Karan was fired from her job. It was a good job, too. In fact, Donna had dropped out of college to take it. It was a job as an assistant at Anne Klein and Company, one of the largest and most successful fashion design companies in New York City. To Donna, who longed to become a famous dress designer, working as an Anne Klein assistant had been a dream come true.

TRYING HARD TO PLEASE

At Anne Klein, they said Donna was just too nervous. It was difficult to blame her since, at age twenty-one, she was assisting some of the most famous and powerful designers in the fashion industry.

Anne Klein (left) works with an assistant on a new design. It was while working at a similar job for Anne Klein that Donna Karan was fired because of her nervous habits. (Harry Benson.)

Donna was an awkward, overeager dreamer with a horsey laugh and a very strong, nasal New York accent. She felt like a complete amateur at her job—like she should know much more about the business than she did.

To make up for her inexperience, Donna tried too hard to please. She ran everywhere at breakneck speed. She talked too fast, stumbling over her words. She bossed other assistants around without meaning to. And to try to demonstrate what good ideas she could come up with for the company, she sometimes even sneaked off to do independent projects without her boss' knowledge or permission. So much clumsiness, combined with Donna's nervous babbling, drove her co-workers crazy.

When things became so bad that Anne Klein couldn't stand to be in the same room with her, Donna began to suspect that her days might be numbered. Of course, worrying about that made her fumble even more. "I couldn't do anything right," she would tell a reporter years later.

But Donna really did many things "right." The real problem was simply that she was still very young, very ambitious, and very much in need of a game plan and some good, down-to-earth advice.

RECOVERY TIME

Donna had always been intensely ambitious. It was a trait noticed by fellow students at the famous Parson's School of Design in New York City, where she attended classes with many of America's future fashion stars. And even before that, when Donna was a not-so-good student at Hewlett High School in Long Island, she would dream big dreams that never really matched her poor grades. Her enthusiasm had put off a lot of people. And if that didn't, her often-voiced fear of failure did.

But *ever* since she was a child, Donna had always believed she'd be *something* when she grew up. Beneath her disorganized, almost comically panic-stricken mask, she hid a sturdy inner resolve that was never completely shaken.

Being fired was embarrassing and scary, but Donna was a survivor. At first she reeled a little from the shock of losing the job she'd waited her whole life to have. But then she became all the more determined to prove she had what it takes to make it in the fashion industry. So she picked herself up and set about deciding what positive things she could do to achieve her goal.

DESIGNING A FASHION CAREER

First, Donna needed to find a new job. Because she had dropped out of Parson's before getting her degree in order to take the job at Anne Klein, job-hunting in New York wasn't as easy as it might have been. There were hundreds of young women much like Donna who also wanted to work for the country's best fashion designers. They, too, dreamed dreams of fashion stardom that were just as far-fetched as her own.

Finally, however, Donna convinced the owner of a little-known sportswear company called Addenda to give her a try. The owner later admitted that she hadn't really wanted to hire Donna. But because the gangly young woman was so charming—and so relentless—she got the job in the end. This was not the first time that Donna's sheer likability and determination would open doors for her that were closed to others. And it wouldn't be the last.

First Trip to Europe

Since Addenda was a much smaller company than Anne Klein, Donna was given more responsibility. Soon she was allowed to run some projects on her own. Working for Addenda, she even got to go on her first buying trip to Europe, a privilege that she would have had to wait years to enjoy at Anne Klein.

In Europe, Donna helped her boss seek out and judge the **fabrics** that would become Addenda fashions later. (Terms in **bold-face type** are defined in the Glossary at the back of this book.) At the same time, she was also able to train her sharp eye on the clothes that European women were wearing.

Donna loved the casual but sophisticated style of women's clothing popular in France and Italy. Unlike the fashion scene in America, European women looked elegant without seeming to try very hard. Their sweaters, skirts, and loose trousers moved freely with them, so that the women looked relaxed and comfortable. Donna made a note that when she became a world-famous designer, she would create clothes with these loose, flowing lines.

If Donna loved European fashions, she was even more delighted with the fabrics that were sold by manufacturers at special, annual shows. Donna had seen luxurious fabrics when she worked at Anne Klein, of course, but never in the quantities she saw on this first trip to Europe.

As she ran her hands over bolt after bolt of custom-dyed silk, suede, and jersey, Donna insisted that the light must be better in Europe because it made her want to just snap up these gorgeous fabrics. By the time she boarded the plane for home, Donna had a clearer idea of what sort of clothing she wanted to design in the future.

Settling Down

Back home in New York, Donna soon took a second step toward directing the course of her life. She married her boyfriend, Mark Karan, the owner of a **boutique** in Brooklyn. As a single woman, Donna had felt a conflict between her unsettled love life and her work that had made her feel she wasn't carrying off either of them very well. Marriage, however, helped settle her down at last so she could concentrate on her work.

Donna was only twenty-two and still rather young to link her life permanently with another person's. But as the daughter of a single-parent family, she enjoyed having a home. And she found that her new role as a married woman helped give her the confidence she needed to make her next, most difficult move.

STARTING OVER

That move took place on a sunny day in 1970, when Donna put on her best clothes, marched back to Anne Klein's offices, and asked to have her old job back. It wasn't easy to return to the building where she had been so embarrassed before. She probably hunched her shoulders a little, dreading the moment when she might run into someone she used to work with, someone who had probably been promoted a time or two in the eighteen months since Donna had been gone.

Nevertheless, Donna returned anyway. She knew that if she was going to achieve her dream, Anne Klein still offered her the best chance to do it. And Donna wasn't a person to back down in the face of a challenge.

Ms. Klein, who was not really surprised to see Donna back

again, admitted that there was an opening for a new assistant. But she pointed out that Donna hadn't been very helpful the first time she had worked there. Donna had to agree, but she convinced her former boss that she had matured since then and now understood what it would take to keep her job.

Anne Klein had always admired Donna's spirit. She decided to rehire the plucky twenty-two-year-old, this time as a non-designing assistant. That meant Donna would start over at rock bottom in the company—making coffee, picking up pins, and drawing charts for the designers. All the people she worked with before would know that she had been demoted.

But Donna didn't complain. This time, she was determined to succeed. She worked longer hours at her new job than the other assistants did and volunteered to help out on projects. She also looked as alert as possible, especially when Anne Klein was around, and learned as much as she could from the older designers she worked for.

Mentors

A mentor is a person more advanced in his or her profession who takes a younger person on as a kind of student, or protégé. This kind of friendship is very helpful for young people just starting out in business. A more experienced person can explain concepts and issues that arise every day that the protégé might not understand. The mentor can point out possible stumbling blocks ahead, and guide the worker through the maze of challenges that often crop up in business relationships.

No matter how good a business education or natural instinct a young person has, it is difficult to become successful without a helpful boost from at least one mentor along the way. Mentors provide the kind of necessary, specific information that doesn't appear in books. Anne Klein, for example, might have gently suggested that Donna would get along with her co-workers better if she toned down her aggressiveness. She might also have shown Donna how to design a blazer to make a woman look more elegant and taller, and many other tricks of the designing trade. And she may have given Donna advice on how to negotiate better pay and conditions with employers in the future.

The mentor relationship is also beneficial to older people. As men and women age, they often develop a desire to pass on what they've learned to the younger generation, so that their many years of experience won't go to waste. Often, mentors see reflections of their younger selves in the eager, ambitious faces of their protégés.

It is very satisfying for successful people to look back and reflect on how they won their business battles. All in all, a mentor-protégé relationship benefits both partners more or less equally. Without mentors, the business world would be much less interesting and enjoyable.

Making a Comeback

In 1971 Donna was rewarded with a promotion to the rank of associate designer. With Anne Klein now guiding and teaching her, Donna began to experiment with some Anne Klein-type designs. She soon came up with some young, original ideas on paper that caught the attention of Tomio Taki, the powerful head of Takihyo, Inc., a Japanese company that owned Anne Klein.

Because she liked the designs so much herself, Donna began to dress the way she drew. She found she loved the convenience and spark of dressing in leotards, tights, and an ever-changing variety of colorful skirts, blouses, and scarves. She studied which combinations worked best, using herself as a model to refine her style.

Working Mother

By the spring of 1974, Donna was hard at work at Anne Klein's side, helping prepare the next year's winter **line.** Though she was pregnant with her first child, Donna worked fifteen- and eighteen-hour days on Anne's designs, practically living at the office.

On March 17, 1974, Donna raced from her office to the hospital to give birth to a girl. She named the baby Gabrielle, after her father, Gabby. While recovering in the hospital, Donna finally had time to take a look at her situation. She reflected that her future indeed looked very bright.

THE TURNING POINT

Then, disaster struck. On March 19, while Donna was still at home recovering from childbirth, Anne Klein died of cancer. The company fell into a turmoil as everyone wondered who would be promoted to take her place. The decision lay with the executives at Takihyo, who were likely to choose an established, already famous designer who would guarantee a return to normalcy right away.

But Tomio Taki kept remembering Donna's designs. Their casual, flowing, flattering lines in feminine fabrics like silk and jersey had struck him as being fresh, simple, and young. They were clothes that women would feel comfortable in and that looked very flattering on them as well. Besides, he reflected, Donna had worked directly with Anne Klein for the past few years. No outsider would understand the Anne Klein look as well as Donna did.

An Unusual Boss

Tomio Taki was a very successful businessman who prided himself on his ability to spot creative talent. Takihyo, the company he headed, was owned by Mr. Taki's family. It had made fabrics for kimonos (Japanese robes) for centuries.

When Mr. Taki decided to buy an American fashion design company, he gathered together ten American women acquaintances. He then gave each of them a huge amount of money, and told them to buy whatever American designer's clothes they had always dreamed of owning.

After the women had bought the clothes, Mr. Taki removed the labels and placed them into separate piles on a table. Anne Klein's labels formed one of the largest piles, so he bought the company.

Mr. Taki's fellow executives knew he often relied on his intuition in business. Still, when he decided to make Donna Karan the chief designer at Anne Klein, most of them were shocked. They objected, saying that at age twenty six, Donna was too young to take over an entire line.

But Mr. Taki believed in Donna, and he trusted his own instincts. Besides, he pointed out, he was only twenty-six when he became president of Takihyo. And with a fifty-percent **interest** in Anne Klein, he was the company's **majority shareholder.** So his decision was final.

DECISION TIME

It was a once-in-a-lifetime opportunity for Donna Karan. But could she live up to it? She was still quite young and inexperienced, and she had never really been an organized type of person. She was also a brand-new mother with a two-day-old child! How could she take on such a big job now?

Then Donna heard the small voice that spoke to her when things got tough: "You can do it, Donna," it said in its broad, New York accent. Although the voice was small, it was stubborn and it wouldn't stop talking. And Donna Karan was smart enough to listen to it.

After all, as Donna later recalled her decision, "I always knew I'd be *something!*"

Chapter 2

Seventh Avenue Baby

When she was little, Donna's parents and their friends called her their Seventh Avenue baby. This was in reference to the garment district on New York City's Seventh Avenue, where both her parents worked.

Donna was born in the suburbs of Long Island, New York, on October 2, 1948. Her father, Gabby Faske, was a tailor, and her mother, Helen Richie Faske, was a beautiful showroom model. Donna and her much older sister, Gail, who would also grow up to work in fashions, were surrounded by industry gossip before they could even talk.

THE EARLY YEARS

As a very small girl, Donna could mimic with ease her parents' comments about hemlines and trouser pleats, about which designers were out and which ones were in. She felt as comfortable watching showroom models display clothes while designers adjusted them as most children her age felt dressing their dolls.

Some of Donna's most vivid childhood memories center around watching her mother model the gorgeous suits, blazers, and skirts that Gabby designed for her. Donna's elegant mother was nicknamed "The Queen" by the family. She liked to dress in bright, glamorous scarves, suits, and turbans. Years later, Donna would be amazed to discover how much her own "new" designs looked like her mother's clothes from those early years.

A Single-Parent Family

But much of Donna's childhood wasn't easy. When she was three, her father died in a car accident. Her mother had to work longer hours in New York City to support the family. She often left for work on the train at dawn and didn't return home until after dark.

Donna admired Helen Faske's strength and determination as she grew older. But as a young girl, she deeply missed the presence of a warm, caring mother, which most children took for granted in those days. As it was, at age 3½, Donna was packed off to her first summer camp just six months after her father's death. She learned to be independent at a very early age.

Donna did not develop into the kind of beauty her mother was. She had long legs like Helen's, but as a growing girl she managed to look more chunky than graceful. It didn't help, either, when her mother decided that they should move to a nicer neighborhood when Donna was seven.

Helen rented a tiny house in the wealthy Long Island town of Woodmere. But Donna didn't feel at all privileged. Instead, she couldn't help but compare her family's lack of money with the obvious wealth of her schoolmates.

In a time when single-parent families were unusual, Donna felt like the only girl on earth without a father. Her sense of being different made her uncomfortable, and she made few friends. The neighborhood boys usually ignored her, except to tease her with the nickname "spaghetti legs."

A Devoted Stepfather

Then, when Donna was around ten years old, her mother remarried. Donna's new stepfather, Harold Flaxman, was in what he jokingly called New York's "schmatte" business—selling cheap copies of fashionable dress designs.

Donna and Harold hit it off right away. The shy young girl began to tell him about the ideas she sometimes had for beautiful clothes. With Harold's enthusiastic encouragement, she began to draw pictures of the clothes whenever she was feeling low.

Harold loved Donna's flowing, ultra-feminine designs. He cheerfully encouraged her to think about becoming a fashion designer. Sometimes he would take her to dinner at Chinese restaurants in the city so they could discuss her future career like two adults.

Once Harold suggested that if Donna wanted to be famous, she should change her name to Ivy Donna (pronounced Do-*nay*), because it sounded fancier. But the young girl just laughed and said that was not her style.

Encouragement from a Friend

Another person who encouraged Donna at that time was Louis Dell'Olio, a classmate of hers at Hewlett High School. Louis wanted to be a designer, too. He and Donna would spend many afternoons after school creating new patterns and experimenting with new ways of piecing them together.

Louis said later that even then he was impressed with the original ways Donna found to cut patterns so that the clothes draped beautifully on the body. She told Louis that when she was very little, she had dreamed of becoming a dancer. Now her love of dance translated into a desire to make flowing, graceful clothes.

The two teenagers encouraged one another about their dreams long before other people noticed or cared about their fashion creations. They became lifelong friends.

FIRST STEPS TOWARD A FASHION CAREER

When she was fourteen, Donna couldn't wait any longer to take her first leap into the fashion industry. Lying about her age, the tall girl, who looked older than she was, landed a job selling clothes at a neighborhood boutique.

Donna would carefully study what sorts of clothes did and didn't look good on the women who came into the store. Just as important, she also noticed that her enthusiasm for clothes was shared by the customers, and she realized that she loved to sell.

The more Donna had to do with fashion, the more obsessed with it she became. Her mother noticed that the high school girl's excitement over anything having to do with clothes was affecting her grades. Design was all Donna talked about, and she began skipping classes in order to study fashion trends at a local mall. Her impatience to get started on her "real," grown-up life was turning her into a rebellious, sometimes difficult teenager.

Fashion School

In 1966, while Donna was finishing her senior year of high school, Helen decided to take matters into her own hands. She asked her boss, himself a fashion designer, to use his influence to help get Donna accepted into Parson's School of Design in New York City. Parson's is one of the best and most respected schools in the country for would-be fashion designers. Helen's boss went to bat for her, and in spite of Donna's unimpressive high school record, she was accepted at Parson's for the following fall.

However, because of her poor high school grades, Donna had to start out on probation at Parson's. This meant that if she failed any classes, she would have to leave school. But she was so thrilled to be at Parson's that she became a model student overnight. Donna started earning excellent grades and never once skipped a class. And the fact that her old friend, Louis Dell'Olio, was also attending Parson's made this first career step even better for Donna.

Fashion designers keep a careful eye on the students at Parson's, hoping to snap up young talent before it becomes very expensive. Several major designers noticed Donna in the two years she attended Parson's. She became known for her humor and originality. But when a job as a summer **intern** at Anne Klein turned into an offer for a permanent position, she dropped out of Parson's and left without looking back.

Nothing could stop Donna now.

Chapter 3

Working Girl

Donna *had* come a long way since her days at Parson's. It was now 1974, she was twenty-six years old, and she had given birth so recently that her ankles were still swollen from her pregnancy. The gangly, zany former assistant had grown up to look like most women's idea of the messier-than-average mom next door.

Now Donna found herself having to put off full-time motherhood in order to create an elegant line of women's clothing that distinctly said "Anne Klein." Moreover, the line had to be unique enough to draw attention to its designer, Donna Karan. This was the chaotic "working-mother" syndrome with a vengeance!

THRIVING ON CHAOS

Fortunately, Donna thrived on chaos. She worked best in a frenzied, hardworking atmosphere mixed with non-stop chatting with her co-workers and assistants that sometimes unleashed some brilliant ideas. She respected her employees and encouraged them to share their thoughts with her. She felt that not only would the company benefit from their creativity, but the employees would enjoy their jobs enough to put in the necessary long hours.

This time around, there was almost more office panic and hysterical laughter than even Donna could really deal well with. But the young mother simply took a deep breath, hired a babysitter, and threw herself into one of the biggest challenges of her life.

Donna ran here and there, pinning up skirts, giving rapid-fire instructions, and taking a few moments every once in a while just to clown around. In the midst of all this hectic activity, she kept asking herself: Now that she had the chance to make a statement with her own designs, what kind of style did she want to tell the world was hers? What kind of designer did she want to be—formal and elegant, young and playful, or exotic and strange? What it all came down to was this: What kind of woman was she designing for?

HITTING ON AN IDEA

Donna let the questions sit for a while. The possibilities were endless, but she was willing to take the time to hit on just the right idea.

Then suddenly, in the middle of Anne Klein's offices, the idea came to her. Donna wanted to create clothes for women like *herself*—working women too busy to shop all over town for dozens of separate outfits as well as purses, handbags, and jewelry to match.

Working women all over America were now engaged in careers that left them little time to spare. They needed clothes they could mix and match—elegant assortments of tights, leotards, sweaters, skirts, and scarves that they could wear one way for the office, then other ways for family time or evening. And Donna was sure the women had money that they'd be willing to spend on such items.

Amazingly enough, fun and versatile designer clothes, aimed at career women instead of socialites, just weren't available in 1974. Perhaps it was because most of the major designers were men. They still thought of the women who could afford their clothes as being mostly rich wives who had nothing to do all day but go to the beauty parlor for manicures and to restyle their hair.

But as a woman herself, Donna realized that such an inactive, wealthy wife was quickly becoming extinct in this country. More often, now, American women who had money had earned it. And women who earned plenty of money had no time or desire to spend long hours each morning and afternoon on their appearance.

Donna believed that her new look might just be a winner. It was a concept original and timely enough to really open a niche in the fashion market and grab the attention of department store **buyers.** It was, in other words, an idea whose moment had come.

A PHENOMENAL SUCCESS

With little time left, Donna expanded on her new idea in the designs for Anne Klein's winter line. Often she brought her baby to the office. The homey atmosphere created by Anne Klein employees stopping to coo and play with Gabby made working as late as midnight more enjoyable.

This was how she liked to work, Donna reflected during a brief pause in her headlong rush to finish the collection in time for Anne Klein's winter show. If she *ever* had her own company, she would arrange it so that family could wander comfortably among employees, and employees could feel like family.

The Show Goes On

Show time finally arrived. Fashion journalists and buyers from across the country, curious about what would become of Anne Klein's company, fought for invitations. Donna ran around frantically, making sure *every* hemline was perfect, and *every* big, bold, bracelet and brooch perfectly suited to the clothes.

Then, one by one, the models began to walk down the runway. A silence fell over the darkened showroom. Backstage, Donna clenched her fists. She thought she would die from the suspense. And then, suddenly, the air was filled with thunderous applause.

Donna's success was phenomenal! Buyers loved her idea of combining separates in easy, sophisticated ways. Takihyo instantly signed Donna to a twelve-year contract before any other hungry design firms could think to steal her away.

Donna had done her homework, though, and she proved to be a tough negotiator. Knowing what she was now worth to the company, she insisted on having almost complete creative control over the styles she would design for Anne Klein's.

How much she would be paid didn't matter much to Donna, but having control over her creations did. Donna was given a green light to expand on what Anne Klein had created and to create her own unforgettable styles.

GOOD FRIENDS AND GOOD TIMES

Donna hired her old friend, Louis Dell'Olio, to design alongside her. Louis knew the kind of look Donna wanted. Soon the two of them were churning out clothes for all seasons that suited Donna's own active, urban, outrageous, and suddenly incredibly popular taste.

Fashion magazines hailed her work, and her designs caused Anne Klein's sales to increase. Takihyo executives realized that Donna really was at the right place at the right time. They had little to do but relax and watch the show.

Over the next ten years, Donna expanded her working-woman design idea throughout Anne Klein. Then, in 1983, with even more success, she introduced Anne Klein II, the company's less expensive sportswear line.

Dell'Olio and Karan had become so successful that the executives at Takihyo decided it was a waste for both of them to work in the same company. Not only was their effort duplicated, but keeping two top designers working on the same line was very expensive because the company had to pay what each of them was worth.

By now, Donna had won three Coty Awards (the "Oscars" of the fashion industry) and had become a member of fashion's Hall of Fame. Tomio Taki decided that the time had come for Donna to branch off with her own company.

After becoming the head designer at Anne Klein, Donna Karan (right) hired her old high school classmate, Louis Dell'Olio (left), to assist her in designing the styles she wanted to create. (Marianne Barcellona.)

FIRED—AGAIN

But Donna couldn't bring herself to give up her job. The pressure of her work and her sudden success had been hard on her marriage, resulting in a divorce in 1983. As a single mother, Donna was afraid to let go of the position that had given her so much security.

And besides, Donna loved working at Anne Klein. Her job had become her obsession (something that is constantly in one's mind), her family, her entire world. She had come to the company as an intern seventeen years ago to prove she could be a good designer, and she had done much more than that. Though Donna did sometimes admit that it would be nice to have the freedom to create a wider range of styles, how could she possibly leave Anne Klein when she was having so much fun?

So Frank Mori, Anne Klein's president, made up Donna's mind for her. In 1983, the same year she was divorced, Donna remarried. Her new husband was Stephan Weiss, a sculptor with two children by a previous marriage. And shortly afterwards, Donna was fired—again. It was the only way Frank Mori could make Donna leave Anne Klein and start her own company.

Chapter 4

Partners

In 1984, with fifty-percent ownership and three million dollars in financing from Takihyo, Donna and her husband started their own company, Donna Karan New York. In addition to Takihyo, Tomio Taki and Frank Mori also joined Donna and her husband as partners in the new venture.

ON THE SPOT

Donna was now on the spot as she had never been before. Not only was her name on the company **logo,** but she knew she was incredibly lucky to be offered three million dollars to start a top-of-the-line fashion business. "People were watching to see where I would mess up," she said later, making a funny face. "Could I *really* do this thing I wanted to do?"

Partnerships

Partnerships in business are much like partnerships in life: two or more people get together and contribute to a joint cause. Often, different partners have different things to contribute, and the percentage of the profits that each partner receives depends on how valuable his or her contribution has been.

For example, Donna Karan's talent was absolutely necessary for the partnership of Donna Karan New York. Without Donna, there would be no company. That's why she received, with her husband, a fifty-percent share in the company. On the other hand, without Takihyo's **investment** of three million dollars, there also would be no company. And that's why Takihyo, Tomio Taki, and Frank Mori together received the other fifty-percent ownership of the company.

Often, in a partnership among people with money and people with talent, the people with money get the larger share. But again, it all depends on how much of value that each partner brings to the business.

Of course, there was no way to find out except to try. Donna named her new company "Donna Karan New York" because she liked its snappy sound, and because "New York" perfectly described her urban, modern, working-woman style. Before she had created

Donna Karan and her partners in Donna Karan New York: from left to right, Frank Mori, Tomio Taki, and her husband, Stephan Weiss. (Fred Conrad/NYT Pictures.)

Despite her busy schedule, Donna tries to find time to spend with her husband Stephan and their three children, Gabby (left) and Lisa and Cory (right). (Marianne Barcellona.)

any clothes to sell, she started work on an advertising campaign featuring herself on a boat near the Statue of Liberty. The idea of the ad was to show that Donna Karan had "arrived"—even if she wasn't yet sure exactly where.

But that was no problem. One of Donna's many mottos is, "Never plan ahead." And it has proven to be a surprisingly useful philosophy in the fashion business. With four major deadlines every year—one every new season—big-time designers have no time to spare for planning ahead. Their energy is best saved for moving through each year one step at a time, planning winter lines while finishing autumn clothes, dreaming up summer clothes right after Christmas, and so on.

Starting at Home

Donna was too impatient to wait for an available showroom to turn up before she started work, so she designed the first fashions for her new company in her own home. Soon the rooms resounded with her harsh accent. "I like that sweater," she would call out, pronouncing it "*sweatuh.*" "Maybe you should try the pink scarf. Yeah, that's it. That's just a-maz-ing!"

Donna found that she actually enjoyed working at home and not having to travel to an office each day. And because she remembered what it was like to have a working mother, she especially enjoyed being around in case Gabby needed her.

But Donna's husband Stephan soon became tired of the crowds of clothes designers camping out in his living room, even if he was one of the company's partners. He finally convinced Donna to move the creative part of the business to another apartment, where she could set her designers up in the living area and use the kitchen as a showroom.

BACK TO BASICS

Faced with the challenge of creating her own line, Donna returned once again to her original idea—the one that had caught on so well at Anne Klein. This time, however, she simplified it to what she called "seven easy pieces" of interchangeable clothing. Then she worked at recalling everything she had learned so far about casual, effortless-looking style and the way clothes flowed in order to make the line look spectacular on the runway.

Perhaps only a woman would have thought to design leotard-type bodyshirts instead of blouses, so that the women who wore them would never have to worry about their shirts riding up. Blazers were designed to match skirts, pants, tights, and scarves, so that an outfit could be switched in an office restroom in the blink of an eye.

Donna, who has described herself as being a little "hippy," had a special knack for using deep, V-shaped necklines and loosely draped clothes to flatter the average woman's body. If the clothes made *her* look sleek and sophisticated, as Donna has often matter-of-factly pointed out, they'd make practically anyone look great.

Once Donna had sketched the basic designs, she went to work on such details as color, fabric, and fit—carefully choosing them to make sure the clothes would move with the body. Donna was glad now that she had spent time in Europe studying fabrics while working for Addenda. She reveled in the choices of fabrics available, and would make several trips to Europe each year to examine custom-dyed materials and order entire lines in a favorite texture or color.

A NEW SELLING IDEA

It was while she was considering fabrics that Donna also rethought the way that clothes were sold in stores. She was the first designer to come up with the "boutique" idea of small stores-within-depart-ment-stores.

In such "boutiques," fashion videos and specially trained salespeople would show customers how to combine various skirts, jackets, and other separates. The salespeople would also help customers choose the appropriate accessories (purses, scarves, etc.) that Donna always displayed with her clothes. Providing entire interchangeable outfits and accessories in one place would save shoppers a lot of time and frustration. Donna was betting that a certain type of woman would pay well for that convenience.

An Important Visitor

Donna's bet paid off. Sonja Caprioni, vice-president of fashion merchandise for the trend-setting I. Magnin department stores based in San Francisco, dropped in at Donna's kitchen showroom one day to see what was going on. Donna showed Sonja a few of her newest creations. The department store executive's expression was impossible to read. Did she like the new look? Did she understand how different outfits could be put together from a few pieces?

Donna was very nervous. She was sure she was talking too much, asking too many questions, and blowing her career. She took a deep breath and smiled as Sonja bid good-bye at the apartment door.

And then Donna waited.

Several days later, the rumors began to fly. Sonja Caprioni, it was whispered, was telling everyone that she loved Donna Karan's new look. In fact, she had been so impressed that she was placing a huge order for the following season's styles.

In the fashion industry, a whisper from such an important buyer is enough to make a designer's career. Soon, orders from stores all over the country started pouring in.

THE FIRST SHOW

Meanwhile, Donna and her employees continued to prepare for her first fashion show. They coordinated different looks, decided on the models, and arranged the order of the **line-up.** They also issued invitations to fashion editors, **retailers,** and other kingpins of the industry who "had the pencil" (fashion lingo for having the power to order clothes for stores). Donna, in the meantime, spent sleepless nights worrying over whether the line would be successful.

But this time, all the effort almost wasn't necessary. The snowball of success that had begun rolling with Donna's first decision to return to Anne Klein was now rolling faster than ever. On May 3, 1985—the night she unveiled her first collection—Donna Karan New York became the hit of the season. Donna received the fashion world's applause with a tingle of excitement and more than a little exhaustion.

Later that year, *Women's Wear Daily,* the leading newspaper of the fashion industry, would call Donna "the hottest designer on Seventh Avenue." Also in 1985, her company launched a line of accessories and a **licensing** division.

Donna's career was made. She would eventually be a rich woman. Donna Karan New York would gross eight million dollars in 1985 (by 1989, the amount would rise to $43 million).

FEELING GOOD

But money was never a big draw for Donna Karan. Much more satisfying was the fact that she felt really good about what she had created. She *liked* the clothes she saw on the runway. She *enjoyed* the competent, powerful, playful and ultra-female image she was offering women. Donna felt proud of the fact that even though Anne Klein had once fired her, she had done all this herself.

That fall, the Bergdorf Goodman department store in New York City staged its first Donna Karan fashion show. By seven o'clock on the evening of the show, the sales of Donna's clothes had broken all store records. That autumn, Bergdorf Goodman's sold more than $250,000 worth of Donna's clothes.

Takihyo's investment had proven to be a good one. But this was only the beginning. Many challenges were yet to come.

Chapter 5

Ups and Downs

Success in life often depends on skill, brains, hard work, and more than a little luck. Donna was creative, clever, and famous for working harder than anyone in her company. But she also turned out to be very lucky, too. It isn't often that a designer is offered three million dollars to start her own company. In both her career and her personal life, Donna Karan ran into more than her share of simple good fortune.

A HELPING FAMILY

First, Donna was lucky with her family, who all pitched in with her to help make her dream come true. Not only did her husband Stephan work as an executive in the company, but Donna's step-daughter, Lisa, modeled Donna's designs. Gabrielle, now a teenager, inspired many fashion lines for younger women. Donna's ex-husband stocked mainly Donna's designs in the two boutiques named after their daughter that he now owned and that were managed by Donna's older sister, Gail Hoffman.

And Lisa's infant daughter, Donna's step-granddaughter, Mackenzi, played the baby in the new Donna Karan "working mother" ads. The ads pictured a woman in dark glasses and Donna Karan clothes juggling a briefcase, a coffee cup, the morning paper, and her baby as she rode to work in the back of a limousine. They were based on Donna Karan's real life, though, of course, they were greatly exaggerated and idealized.

Donna loved having her family involved in her working life. For one thing, it was the only way she got to see them. She is a warm, affectionate woman who would have enjoyed spending more time at home if her craving for the fashion world hadn't claimed her.

As it was, the fitting rooms at company headquarters took on the atmosphere of the living room at home. While Donna and her daughter squabbled over styles, Lisa played at mixing and matching various bits of clothing as baby Mackenzi crawled over the furniture. In the meantime, assistants, designers, photographers, and even Donna's husband breezed casually in and out.

"Adopted" Family

And if Donna's workers weren't already part of her family, they were usually "adopted" soon enough. She was surrounded by friends, including Patti Cohen, her publicity director. Patti was an old friend whom Donna had hired because she believed in her potential, though she knew Patti had no previous experience.

Even the department store buyers, photographers, and magazine editors she dealt with through business became longtime friends of Donna. She was just the type of person people wanted to do things for, a personable quality that was a big advantage in her career.

A Life of Constant Pressure

All in all, it was an ideal life for Donna, even if the stress of every seasonal show proved overwhelming at times. One of the difficulties of a fashion career is that one's work is judged every few months. A designer can be a wild success at the winter fashion shows, but if his or her spring and summer lines bomb, that designer may be out of a job.

Many designers might have folded under the constant pressure of Donna's life, and many families might have resented and rebelled against it. But, so far at least, her family's sense of humor and Stephan's ability to force Donna to relax have given them all a reliable safety release.

Donna was also incredibly lucky in that not many designers—even great ones—are offered three million dollars to invest in their careers. And very few are made chief executive officers of companies bearing their names.

Most designers who break out on their own must start small and build their businesses gradually. Donna had the chance to start big. Of course, that chance carried with it the possibility of failing big as well.

STUMBLING BLOCKS

In the late 1980s, while teaching herself how to run a fashion business, Donna managed to stumble more than once. When her own ideas created problems for the company, she had to learn quickly how to deal with them before they got out of hand.

Selling an Idea

Donna's idea for "boutiques" in department stores was so daring that at first no stores would try it. In fact, department store owners were appalled at her demand for areas of floor space devoted exclusively to her clothes. Floor space is considered a store's most valuable **asset.** What if Donna's clothes didn't sell? A certain amount of floor space would fail to pay for itself.

Donna had to demonstrate how setting aside space for her line alone would allow her to show women how to wear her clothes—and would pay off handsomely in time for the store. Women would grow to depend on the "boutiques" as fashionable one-stop outfitters, she explained, and would quickly come back for more. The boutiques would be time-savers for busy working women. And with such women, time-savers attract more spending than anything else.

At first, Donna insisted on having floor space set aside for a Donna Karan boutique. She even threatened not to sell her clothes to stores that wouldn't give space to her. But when several stores refused to go along with the idea, Donna sheepishly let them sell her clothes anyway.

In the end, Donna's loss of face didn't matter much. Word soon spread about her mix-and-match designs. Her clothes began to sell so well that stores that had refused her space gladly offered it to her now—if she would let them buy more of her clothes!

Late Deliveries

Other problems did not disappear so easily, though. In the early years of Donna's new company, a number of fabric manufacturers failed to deliver their goods on time. As a result, **production** fell behind, and Donna had a hard time delivering her clothes by the date promised.

On top of that, Donna's first design lines were too successful! Because the expected retail sales jumped from four million dollars to six million dollars the first year, it was hard to keep up with the demand. Deliveries began to fall behind more and more often, and Donna faced the possibility that stores would soon start canceling their accounts.

Donna needed cash to buy more fabrics and manufacture more clothes—*fast.* "You cannot make it without the financial backing," she explains. "You need money to make money."

For many **entrepreneurs,** the lack of **capital** to finance expansion can mean failure. But again, Donna was lucky. Takihyo was willing to invest millions more in her company. In fact, Takihyo put another seven million dollars into Donna Karan New York over the next three years.

Capitalization

Capitalization is simply the process of providing money, or capital, to start or expand a business. Donna Karan emphasizes the importance of proper capitalization because so many people eager to start a company blind themselves to how expensive it will really be.

Of course, everyone makes a list of possible expenses and tries to raise enough capital to keep the business going without a profit for a reasonable length of time. But often, they neglect to figure in enough money for the hidden or unexpected expenses that always crop up.

Such expenses might be higher than expected utility (electricity, heat, etc.) bills, over-time wages for employees, or an increase in the cost of supplies. And if customers are late making payments, shortages in cash might occur. Even if a certain amount of extra money is budgeted for such emergencies, other unexpected emergencies can come up.

In a world in which most new businesses fail, a lack of sufficient capitalization, even when a company's level of business is fantastic, is a major pitfall.

Problems with Fabrics

Sometimes, Donna's own love of interesting, unique fabrics got her company into hot water. Her competitors love to talk about the times Donna designed clothes in fabrics so luxurious and expensive—like baby llama or a deluxe cashmere—that even her wealthy customers wouldn't buy them.

Another time Donna **imported** a beautiful gold-threaded cloth from Italy that later proved impossible to sew. And once two fabrics she ordered dyed in the same shade of pink in Europe arrived in two completely different shades—threatening to ruin another line of clothes.

Saying No to Barbra

Then there was the time Donna designed some chenille sweaters that she liked so much she often wore them herself. (Donna never wears any clothes but those she has designed, believing that if she won't wear them, she can't expect other women to.) One day, while in the middle of a heated conversation, she dropped a cigarette ash on the sweater she was wearing and the fabric instantly caught on fire.

Donna managed to put the fire out with no serious damage to herself. She immediately ordered the sweaters withdrawn, but the worst was yet to come. The next day she received a call from Barbra Streisand, who had wanted to buy a chenille sweater but couldn't find one. Could she please buy one from Donna directly?

Donna had to say no. She idolized Barbra Streisand. If the singer burned up in one of Donna's sweaters, Donna would never forgive herself! It was one of the most difficult refusals Donna had to stick to in her career.

"Accent the positive, delete the negative," became Donna's motto in both her clothing designs and her career. Meanwhile, she learned to keep her eye on the **bottom line,** studying how each design fared on the selling floor.

Chapter 6

Major Expansion

In 1988, as her business continued to grow, Donna heard her daughter Gabby complain that none of her mother's clothes fit her. Donna thereupon came up with her best inspiration yet: DKNY. This is a lower-priced line for younger women who like Donna's styles but can't afford her more expensive designs and prefer their clothes a little more casual.

The DKNY line was displayed in Donna's department store boutiques along with her other clothes, but it far outsold the higher-priced line from the very first year. While most new designers hope for a good **sell-through** within six to eight weeks, some of Donna's new designs sold out on the first day. DKNY was proclaimed "the runaway hit of the decade."

Donna was ecstatic over her new line's success, though she worried about the extra work it would mean for her. Basically, with

Photographers take pictures of a happy Donna Karan in her showroom after the fashion show in which she introduced her DKNY line. (Harry Benson.)

DKNY she had doubled the size of her company. But an enormous increase in company income also meant having to spend much more time at the office. Though she regretted not being able to take more vacations, DKNY was too enjoyable an enterprise for Donna to give up.

An Ability to Sell

Much of Donna's success was due to her natural sales ability. It was an ability that Donna discovered she had decades ago as a fourteen-year-old salesgirl in a Long Island boutique. "Donna could sell anything," a friend once remarked.

By 1988, Donna didn't just have a fashion following. It was more like "a super fashion cult." In fact, Donna had a reputation as a kind of general cheerleader for whatever needed cheering. She encouraged her assistants to marry their boyfriends and settle down, and she advised perfect strangers to undertake exercise programs. ("You can do it! I know you can!" she would tell them.)

It was as though Donna's enthusiasm constantly overflowed its bounds. She rarely walked if she could run, she never talked if she could shout. And if she could encourage even one other human being to join her in a spirited exchange of jokes or ideas, she was in Donna Karan heaven.

But Donna's real genius, her clients agreed, was her ability to *communicate* what she envisioned to the head of a store, to a buyer, and to a customer. With her oversized glasses and long, dark ponytail, she looked like every woman's college roommate. Who could resist her confident voice insisting that suede was the fabric of the eighties, even if five minutes ago one hated suede? If Donna hadn't made millions in fashion, said her friends, she would have made millions selling something else.

Selling to Celebrities

Donna would add that she truly loved comfortable, stylish clothes—particularly *her* clothes. And she loved helping women look and feel as beautiful as they possibly could. She was so enthusiastic about selling her designs that once, at a fashion show at Bergdorf Goodman's, she actually sold the clothes off her back to television journalist Barbara Walters. She changed out of the clothes in the ladies' room and had to go home in a robe.

Other famous women who have bought Donna's creations include another TV journalist, Diane Sawyer, and actress Candice Bergen of the TV show "Murphy Brown." These celebrities chose Donna Karan's clothes because they were attractive and needed a minimum of fuss. (They also respect and identify with the designer, who works as hard as they do and is in at least as much demand.) By simply wearing Donna's clothes in front of a camera, these clients increase the demand for the designs enormously. In fact, Donna's clothes are now often referred to as the "Murphy Brown" look!

COMPANY CHANGES

The success of the DKNY line meant that Donna Karan New York had to transform itself from a loose, family-type operation to a more structured company. Stephan resigned, preferring to spend his time sculpting and trying to get Donna to relax. Not that this was very likely, however. Though she was a little saddened by the increasing formality at work, Donna understood that it was necessary in order to control such a wide-ranging group of interests.

Of course, Donna herself still joked with assistants as she helped pin up hems and replace missing shoulder pads. And daughter Gabby still wandered in once in a while, sometimes just to borrow an outfit for a dance.

But, in general, just as Donna had grown up while working in design, so her company had grown up, too. Determined to stick to her vision even as the company expanded, Donna learned to assign many of the business decisions to the competent people she had hired. But she kept the creative "fun part" of designing for herself. In recognition of her fashion creations, in 1990 Donna was named Women's Designer of the Year by the Council of Fashion Designers of America.

By 1991, only six years after Donna Karan New York began, it employed 350 people and its **projected earnings** for the year were more than $150 million. These earnings came not only from the company's basic collection and from DKNY, but also from the **royalties** brought in by the licensing of the Donna Karan name to the manufacturers of eyeglasses, jewelry, sewing patterns, shoes, hosiery, and furs. And in 1990, projected earnings also included Donna's newest creation, DKNY Jeans—the only jeans that fit *Donna* right!

Royalties

A successful designer generates a great deal of money from the number of clothes he or she sells. But if his or her designs prove consistently popular, the designer also creates an even more valuable item: a company **trademark.** The trademark, or name of the design line (Donna Karan New York, for example, or DKNY), is a sign of quality to the customers who buy that product.

If the customers like what they have seen or bought in the past, they are much more likely to pay for an item if that trademark is stamped somewhere on it. Manufacturers of sunglasses, purses, furs, and other items will pay enormous amounts of money, or royalties, for the right to use the Donna Karan trademark. The name "Donna Karan" on their product greatly increases their chances of making a very large profit.

A manufacturer, or "licensee," pays Donna Karan New York perhaps $250,000 for the right to hold the license (that is, use the company's trademark) on its products for a year. It also pays a royalty of five to seven percent of its gross earnings—earnings before production and other expenses are subtracted from income—from products bearing Karan's name. Of course, the designer has to keep a careful eye on the products to make sure they're made well enough to live up to the Donna Karan name.

Bergdorf Goodman's in Manhattan recently built a 1,500-square-foot luxury boutique to display Donna Karan New York. Twice a year, Donna herself demonstrates her new line of clothes to wealthy women at Bergdorf's, and brings in at least $400,000 in revenues while she's at it.

INTERNATIONAL MARKETS

Donna's fashions have gone international as well. Her designs are now sold in London and Tokyo, with more markets always on the horizon. Even French women, perhaps the same women whose fashions Donna had admired twenty years ago, are being seen in her clothes. As any American designer knows, French women don't take to foreign fashions lightly.

And what is Donna thinking during all of this? She's thinking about the next season's fashions. As you read these words, this may well be what's going through Donna's head: "Denim. Now, denim is a wonderful fabric to style."

Chapter 7

An American Dream

With all the magazine articles, ads, television coverage, and other attention Donna Karan has enjoyed, people who don't know her might think of the ground-breaking fashion designer as some kind of glamour queen. However, nothing could be farther from the truth.

Donna's now a multi-millionaire and her evenings, when she's not working, are often spent at gala New York social events or riding in her chauffeured car and drawing a crowd of admiring clients. But at heart, forty-something Donna is still the same funny, overworked, constantly frazzled wife, mom, and career woman with the eternally messy desk that she has always been.

"I was never in this for the glamour," Donna once told an interviewer, thinking back, perhaps, to her lonely childhood as an unpopular Long Island girl. "This is not a glamorous profession. It's an obsession. You don't become a designer. You can't help it."

Donna is a disorganized dreamer who managed to turn herself around when the time came for her to do so. She knows all

Donna Karan is being applauded after a successful showing of her fashions for the spring of 1990, the year in which she was named Women's Designer of the Year by the Council of Fashion Designers of America. (Peter L. Gould/Images, Inc.)

about hard work and obsession. They've brought her riches and fame. And when she can tear herself away from the business long enough to enjoy her family—of both relatives and friends—they've brought her immense happiness as well.

"She made it come true with wishing," says Patti Cappalli, her former boss at Addenda and still one of Donna's closest friends. "But hers is the adult version of the American dream; you know, where you make it after years of slaving, not by being discovered in the mailroom."

Donna wouldn't trade this dream for any other in the world.

Glossary

asset   Something of value that belongs to a person or company.

bottom line   How much something really costs, with all expenses figured in.

boutique   A small clothing store.

buyers   The people who order items for stores.

capital   Money, goods, or property used to produce an income.

entrepreneur   A person who organizes, controls, and takes all the risks of running a business.

fabrics   Materials that clothing is made from—everything from leather to linen.

import   Bring something into the United States from a foreign country.

interest   The portion of a company that a shareholder owns.

intern   A student or other beginner who works at a company for free in exchange for hands-on experience.

investment   Money put into something in order to make more money in the future.

licensing   Selling a manufacturer the right to use a designer's name on the goods he manufactures and sells, in exchange for an agreed-upon payment.

line   The collection of clothes a designer creates for each season.

line-up   The order in which fashions are modeled in a fashion show.

logo   A unique symbol that identifies a specific company or product.

majority shareholder   The person who owns the largest percentage of a company, and therefore has the most say in how it will be run.

production   The process of manufacturing something.

projected earnings   The amount of money a company expects to earn within a certain amount of time—for example, the next year.

retailer   A person who sells goods to the general public.

royalty   An amount of money paid by an organization that has the right (license) to use or sell a work (book, piece of music, play, etc.), name (trademark), or product that is owned by an individual or another organization.

sell-through   The time it takes for a product to finish selling in stores.

trademark   The legally registered name of a company or product.